THE DAUGHTER INDUSTRY

SOHAM PATEL

THE DAUGHTER INDUSTRY

A HAUNTOLOGICAL CONFESSION
ALTERNATIVE HISTORY
SPECULATIVE AUTOPOETICS
IN THREE ACTS
WITH SEVEN PLAYERS

NIGHTBOAT BOOKS
NEW YORK

Printed in the United States

ISBN: 978-1-643-62308-5

Design and typesetting by Kit Schluter
Typeset in EB Garamond and Fjalla One

Cover art:
Detail from *Cabbages, a "Wigglemuch" design*,
by Herbert E. Crowley, circa 1910,
The Metropolitan Museum of Art, New York.

Cataloging-in-publication data is available
from the Library of Congress

Nightboat Books
New York
www.nightboat.org

FOR OM, JORGE, JACK, JACKSON, AND DAD

CONTENTS

ACT I

ACT II

ACT III

PLAYERS

SAI: *The Divine Person Akin to Being a God*—Virgoish and moody. An intense boi or sissy or boy or butch who is indecent, uninhibited, yet rigid with restraint. Sai is pouty and assertive. Oftentimes he is whispersinging sometimes like a heartrending auncle or uncle sometimes like a gossiping aunty oftentimes he rolls his eyes while reciting his lines. Sai's never tired.

SAJANI: *Beloved*—Venerated femme mother who is very bold partly because she would've read all Toni Morrison's contributions to the world partly because of her own mother's strength and partly due to a Scorpio sun sign she would've been born under. Sajani wears purple-colored clothes and makeup. She has a deep voice. Her hallux is shorter than her second toe. At her matrimonial varmala exchange she'd garland the bridegroom first as he'd quickly bow his head to her.

SUVALI: *Full of Grace*—With an elegance akin to Sajani's matriarchal calm, Suvali is a trifle higher femme and Sagittarius maybe none of these players know a birth date for real they're all unborn ghosts you know. Suvali wears lots of gold and is draped in pale linens while her head is wrapped in a bright greenish-blue sarong. Underneath, her hair is long. On each hand, innumerable and deep palmar flexion creases.

SASMITA: *Always Laughing*—Playful, often irreverent and if born, a serious Leo who'd celebrate a birthday daily or on each hour even. Sasmita is limber, genderfluid, jester-like and, of course, always laughing. She/They too frequently sing and dance with Sheetal. If Sasmita had a record label it would be called "Laugh It Off Music Group, Incorporated." Her posture throws her shoulders back high, confidently poised, lion-like, cobra-strong.

SHASHA/SHEETAL: *Moon/Cool*—They maybe would be Gemini and their

voices/bodies express percussive performative energy. They'd have OK Cupid Biodata. Shasha wears thick black eyeglasses and has a profoundly stable strength that waxes and wanes (like the moon)/Sheetal is cool and wears an ornately embroidered vest with gold and silver thread, has distinct facial hair, and is oftentimes also dancing with Sasmita.
*NOTE: SHASHA/SHEETAL can be one player or two.

SARAH: *Princess*—Darkly transcendent and tall, hooded and likely a heavenly Pisces (understand again every day is all of their birthdays and we will celebrate!) abstract and airy with deeply studied skills, rooted knowledges. Sarah is luminous, has a tiara of course and fairy lights sewn into the fabrics of her clothes. Her hand is promised to a prince who is also her friend.

SIDHANGANA: *Divine/Pure*—Chorus
*NOTE: SIDHANGANA is sometimes called SID.

THE DAUGHTER INDUSTRY

IN MY DOTTED SUIT AND NO DUPATTA

On one of the days I found my gender I was in my white dotted orange Punjabi suit sans dupatta I always went sans dupatta because a dean at the arts college told me I had to wear the dupatta always while working and when I asked him why he said to me with smiling eyes in his third language and my first and only fluent one "So you always look like a pretty girl!" I remember a taxi ride to the airport to fly from I think somewhere in the south back north I was studying literatures and music and yoga while visiting family teaching and traveling in between and also I was on a quest to revisit places I read when reading *The God of Small Things* so yes maybe I was near Cochin flying out in the morning now I remember it was morning because the hostel's taximan also took a neighbor girl to her school she got in the back seat with me there at the hostel where I was staying when she got out at her school for some reason one being I hadn't yet found my gender the taximan I think had been watching me for days traveling solo in my twenties no dupatta walking freely from museums to cathedrals to bookshops to beach playing chess and drinking whisky with the local boys who'd slap me in the face for making stupid moves with my knights and rooks and going home to masturbate alone in my room for hours before passing out he watched me do this for days and knew I think now maybe he knew too I hadn't yet found my gender I got in the front seat next to him for the rest of the ride to the airport and it was breezy we stopped for chai and paan and only when we turned to the road with nothing else on it maybe one mile long to the terminal did I realize I had put myself into a bad situation he started to tell me about my body how I need to build it to show status then pinched my tricep gently I in a shock froze even though everything even Roy's writing and mom's rage as warning said don't go here so he didn't stop his fingers continued to my leg muscles feeling somewhere between massage and incorrect he reached his long lean arm under my suit top and cupped my left one i felt my nipple harden on his palm's cool skin and he left it there all the way to departures where he parked and tried to go under my pants but I stopped his hand and held it on top of my clothes for like a minute and after getting out I leaned my hip into his shoulder as he counted change for my fare and handed me the bills before I walked away he pulled me back in and said (and was right) "Don't worry sex is coming coming coming!" I ordered a Kingfisher pint in the airport lounge and was underserved by the slim mustachioed man who explained to me that drinking full pints is not lady-like so I ordered three more then took small sips from each glass then gulped it all down like a rushed microbrew flight before boarding cuz I knew all of it from the burps to the buzz would feel good and give me lift

STUDY (I)[∞]

Sen says "Shankaracharya the philosopher and educator who lived during AD 788-200 set up centers of study and worship and indeed, as early as 1817, the young queen of Travancore said that by diffusion of the education the people they might be better subjects and public servants

Sen says it is often said that women make up a majority of the world's population. They do not

Sen says similar neglect of women's health care and medical attention vis-à-vis men can be seen also in many other parts of the world

Sen says see *Hunger and Public Action* see Wolf's *Revolution Postponed* (1984)

Sen says the responsibility system and perceptual distortions are a variant of what Marx had called "false perception," in family productions

Sen says such as a higher likelihood that men will die from violence, for example, and from diseases related to smoking

Sen says in this context it is also useful to compare ratios of birth and ratios of women in legislature

Sen says statistical yearbooks show a steady decline in the already very low ratio of women to men in the population, from 94.32 in 1979 to 93.42 in 1985 and 1986 it has risen since then, to 93.98 in 1989—still lower than what it was in 1979

∞ December 20, 1990 issue of *The New York Review of Books*. Amartya Sen "More Than 100 Million Women Are Missing."

Sen says gainful employment is not the only factor affecting women's chances of survival

Sen says the responsibility system Sen says see World Bank's World Development Reports Sen says an assessment of the available evidence can be found Sen says the mistaken belief is based on generalizing and how can we understand, explain these differences, respond to them? Sen says at birth boys outnumber girls everywhere in the world there are 105 or 106 male children for every 100 female children Sen says considerable research Sen says resistant to disease Sen says even in the womb Sen says promotion to senior executive positions Sen says basic nutrition and health care Sen says enjoyed by women evolutionary links influencing well-being interesting investigations other aspects of the problem are discussed more extensively first documented in 1975 quantifying trends in conditional ratios the practices of parental sex discernment sperm wash property ownership

Sen says on this and related matters Sen says see case studies see Banister, Stern, Hussain, Cole, Bardhan, Dréze, Boserup, Agarwal, Ahmad, Kynch, Chen, Miller, Bardhan again, Jain, Banerjee, Harris, Watson, Momsen, Townsend, Gupta, more Banister, Tinker, Papanek, Boserup, Avebury/Gower, Johansson, Waldron et al.

ACT 1
earthwater

In an antipatriarchal culture males do not have to prove their value and worth. They know from birth that simply being gives them value, the right to be cherished and loved.

—bell hooks
The Will to Change: Men, Masculinity, and Love

ROLE CALL

(Players do yoga)

SAJANI: Beloved—and the sound of a singing bowl

SUPRIYA: Well-loved—Tina Turner's "What's Love Got to Do with It"

SARA: Precious—sound roses make when growing in a garden

SARAH: Princess—Yo-Yo Ma on a Bach cello suite

SAI: The Divine Person Akin to Being a God—staccato triangle strikes

SIDHANGANA: Divine/Pure—the sound of silence

SAROJINI: In the lotus—heavy breathing

SHASHA: Moon—whatever the moon sounds like

SHEETAL: Cool—windchimes (bamboo)

SASMITA: Always Laughing—hahajajalolz

SHAIVI: Prosperity—plastics

SHUSHMA: Fragrant—Prince's *Purple Rain* live on vinyl recorded in mono

SINJINI: Sound of anklet—sound of anklet

SUVALI: Full of Grace—and exhale OM

SAI TELLS A GHOST STORY

(while practicing some version of surya namaskar aka sun salutations)

One morning in late 2010 I looked out my apartment window in Pittsburgh where I always saw a parking lot, the Spinning Plate Artist Lofts, and a euonymus-lined part of the avenue, there at the beginning of Friendship.

I knew all the families living on the block because of the rescue dog I live with—we would walk around and routinely meet the people.

That early morning and only that morning, I thought I saw or I saw out the window a figure of what seemed to be a like four or five-year-old brown girl riding a bicycle up Friendship Avenue then fade away.

How else I know I saw a ghost is the child seemed so composed, happy, and it was way too early in the morning for someone so young to be out riding alone.

GHOSTS GOSSIP AS THEY MASSAGE EACH OTHER'S EXTREMITIES

SAJANI: So fast at long last what can be catched?

SUVALI: This industry takes place at times on a surgical stage.

SASMITA: In a theatre where a boy is born: sweets for the whole town!

SHASHA: As for the arrival of the girlchild, everyone will ask also if you knew it was so in gravidity.

SHEETAL: But keep if you can a butter knife near the cinnamon. Snip the stick's bottom. Leave all the lights on during centurion procedures. Top the tension with whiskey.

SASMITA: Disguise her life likened to a cat, a groundling, or with two hands held together see how the shadow becomes a doggie?

SARAH: Brother's songs always linger like a sister can't light the pyre or sweep gravestones.

SUVALI: Like a girl can't burn incense for the living & dead so they won't be in between so they're ok not in limbo amid borders in which space shall we live to be here?

SASMITA PROPOSES

Here's to the machines made to say enough now:
Cheers! What are you having? A boy or an abortion?

A machine to look inside: it's the ultrasound
waves bouncing in the interior & no radiation!

Shatter sound pumps heart stutter haha heart stutter.
Price of reveal party is one more U.S. west coast inferno.

Womb as a landing and wound. A worker's co-pay in cash
only and the confetti from the cannon's only pink or blue.

Profit when box we tick's from S to M so announce the auspicious
event! We'll eat toasts and there will be cake. A dance number

is in the works slide shows we'll electric slide in our electric
shoes after we find where our nephews nieces niblings hid them.

PRINCESS IN A SEQUIN DRESS PIROUETTES

if given a chance to pick another time and place to live in i still pick this

only since we have not yet imagined new tradition conceiving modes

our critical force can hold over to novel meanings in the sound of heart

a heart that beats both into its very own stumble and into its very own stop

trace any labor in sweat equity over time on the floor overtime pocket change PTO

I don't mind working so hard if it means our kids won't have to though they'll have

To fight for water as the current climate collapse continues sinking our turtle earth ship

We are in a genocide and we live in genocide we live during a genocide and with this gendercide

We live when Christmas's cancelled in Bethlehem then famine and polio no feasts for after the fasts

Children wail on laptop's livestream while I weep dead sea salts dissolve in bathtub water with me

I weep and I will sing and dance I will spin and sparkle with you even when there's no need to

MOON SKIPS IN THE FIELD WITH WAVING AND OUTSTRETCHED ARMS

send adolescents to the market sell futures in newspaper classifieds

NRI winter trip to motherland for wedding bride shopping roll

out the barrel we'll have a lot of fun see seven girls in one week!

son of a Modi bro rajabheta's biodata for ex. there is none! Rdo

has faith singing to the tune of TLC's "Waterfalls" (*hums the tune*)

new ballads so young Barron relinquishes patrilineal evils! in orange

theory class we flirt with soft butch coach contract discounts

on club membership! forecast advisements! conjugal production!

wills to assure management of wealth land trust property made

some arrangements well with a stable there's money in horses!

SASMITA'S ALWAYS LAUGHING

In joy the doctor takes his tea in the evenings.

"Slapping the father on the back and saying, 'you're a lucky man' is hint enough "In 2003-5 the figure was 880 girls born per 1,000 boys "In 2004-6, that had risen to 892 "And in 2006-8 to 904

Between ration and boiling and milk and sugar his books line the floor. Birth child bachelor master wedding day but saying say uncle began when?!

All the wallas are making clothing out of cloth that will be washed.

paper dolls coral slugs mother
land no man's land spay to spayed
monarch wings rose to power

points crack me up

(in Actualities) a
horse is a horse
declares go home no
no corporate author-
ity makes the crown
and the crowd want
to take down notes

COOL/MOON DRAWS BIRTH CHARTS

their skin's translucent and less so when exposed to air they're waiting in numbers dropped off in front of government buildings in a bundle here comes love here comes marriage there once was a girl named ________________ they are all lost in the supernovas possibly they kiss in the orphanage where rows of full-size beds line up empty they are a generation now crossing over to the sky instead

their skin erupts and itches less from the eczema when they can eat well and in the winter months it's less lush but they can eat well and completely in any season with an abundance of seasonings they inject their skin with drugs and medicine and when alive they are so much so it's so contagious it could rise the dead jolt us up again when they're not it's a zero hole healing to fall into each night

their skin's electric with light and refraction a glow soft ripple into the atmosphere worn bare with cashmere gold ornaments and tattoos of animals objects and other messages channeling ancestry once again for the promises of investment their skin's been cut open from a fall and slips wax burned for play they step inside shadows stop and bliss comes when they are reading their stars

BELOVED WRITES A LETTER

You are no singular existence here. The year: 1982. We watch *E.T.* in a movie theater and even though the theater is full of people you are the only one in the room with me.

In a memory of this moment.   I hear children snore over playhouse loudspeakers. We smell less the smell of butter flavor and our shiny candies and more the lingering smell of smoking is allowed from decades ago. After several years what seems possible is this: you alive with me. Sitting in darkness, our sticky floor pushes up against layers of rubber and canvas on our shoes and then on my jeaned knees and then on the palms of your hands that you will later lick for the salt taste.

In the movie there is a boy on a bicycle. The eponymous extraterrestrial character sits wrapped in a blanket in a basket mounted on handlebars. They fly on the bike in front of the moon. When I ask you what you remember you say we were eating the same candy the boy used to lure the alien. You picked some up off the ground and put the pieces in your mouth. E.T. needs help from Elliott to go home, to be lifted into the sky, to disappear. You too blur into space.

Amniocentesis was introduced around 1974 so now in the science of living bodies: regarding birthing, blood flow in the umbilical cord and placenta can be observed with real-time sonography. And we know now a camera can sound a heartbeat, show a throb. We see shimmer against hospital white and that glossed monitor   in cystic spaces: a pattern   pulsatile, whirling and accelerated flow

visible even to suggest a death.   When I ask you if it is conceivable: to graph a function of space in which intuition could take the place of the screen you say yes.

There is a frequency that keeps the body alive. You keep that metal whistle you won at the fair around your neck. I have never heard you blow into it but sometimes the wind is enough to make it make a sound. Because to know you would be to know how to answer a question I do not know how to ask: what I am wishing is an open sky for you—and there is one with new planets forming a brilliant and almost blinding blue light.

SEALS ENVELOPE WITH SPIT

Years later, we hear once upon a time once more when mother tells us:
The rain it did not stop for the whole month of June after which the wind

Switched then drought and then mewing calls from peafowls:
Indian, Green, and White. We were not afraid. We could taste

The river water lifted into the air. And still the rain did not stop.
We were not afraid because some bridges we could swim under.

During certain evenings we could feel like riverbeds almost floating river-
bank crops harvest and meats have a certain use for soup for sureness's

Selection's so natural churn milk stocks to butter the fields become kitchen.
Eat eat then sleep goodnight we all write a survival story down somewhere.

SWARA: Music—hipster t-shirts
SYUH: Can exist—a beam of light
SATVI: Existence—bad posture from gender bending
SVEDA: Born from sweat—hot all the time
SATYA: Truth—would've been an engineer
SHALYACHIKITSAKAH: Surgeon—surgeon
SAVRITI: Mother—MILF
SHAILI: Tradition—visa pass port green cards
SAURA: Celestial—gold bullion factories bitcoin
SIVANI: Suture—birth right citizen

DEBENTURES (FULL OF GRACE)

eyelid kisses

the glass larynx

opens for breath

a drink of water

skin sheds

blessings for every hair

wings bloodied

on backwards hawks

sounds of a light's beam

i am in the sky

you are there singing

in between pulsings

of a wingspan's flap

sounds of guts falling

to the floor before dog

licks up mess in her mouth

then clean quiet hum om

in the garden or the act

ends as origins as horses

resemble us, my loves our

limited partnership interest

provides life we can imagine

EVERYONE FLICKERS
(CHORUS)

One pack whisky for each daughter
    gives me tension tops
    attention over primers

Now marry them off
    then entitled domain

Field acres for
    mango/marijuana
    grazing
    barley/tobacco/ba
    nana

For camels and gold
    a ring of gold enough to bury

Any villain we
    have all been good

Cacka is uncle
    and shit and bird
    screech both Cacka
        Cacka Cacka

Busted faces force-fed
unhulled rice punctures
windpipes

stripped thrift
                    fertilizer
stinks girl birth
burdens   a
blueshift kill

lingers on suf-
focated lungskin
to thrill throttle
ring and roar

fire on dried milk w/saf-
fron singes the air

SAJANI'S SPINAL TWIST

Burden wills on as
I (r)age blazed
power and the dark.
Blissful sleep drool
in my sleeve. What's
left of the dancer's
dress? What world
can have us happy?
The day gets long
and years larger.
Many men hinge
to ennui with flashed
matches and tobacco
for pipes hold alert
virtues to stir often
enough and shrug
any wrongdoing
into good like
skin cooled
on polished marble
in the heat's hot
afternoon. Or to
bite into an apple
and look up to a sky's
blue. Morning forever
can offer new fruits.

IN UNISON

SHALULU: Perfume—mifepristone pitocin
SHAFALI: Fragrant—misoprostol
SHAHNTI: Peace—gestational ages
SHANTHI: Peace—prostaglandin E1
SHANTI: Peace—hemabate ampoule
SHARI: Arrow—dinoprostone miscellaneous
SHEELA: Character—carboprost tromethamine
SHANTIH: Shantih shantih shantih—oxytocin

WHISPERS IN A GAME OF TELEPHONE

SUVALI's mouth near Sajani's ear: "a daughter killer myself, I ask to know the gender during daughter in-law's ultrasounds...

SAJANI to Sarah: "she came into the family by my blessing I made my son a doctor and made him marry...

SARAH to Sheetal: "marry who I say he can and exactly when and I ask even at my own daughter's doctor visits...

SHEETAL to Shasha: "who wants to bring another girl into this world she will be so costly to us and a further curse...

SHASHA to Sasmita: "when I look for wife for my own son it is also just because I want lower blood pressure and a friend...

SASMITA to Suvali: "only she can't be more educated than me respectability is just so very important to me with my de-man-ding/family...

SUVALI to Sai: "aaaaaaachaaa! she will inevitably belong to us as I am my father's daughter industry and also my mother in-law's I am hers as well and any-way...

SAI off into to the middle distance: "and any-way I am now alive to tell this story that has to be worth at least some-thing...

ACT II
firewater

But I, like other queer people, am two in one body, both male and female. I am the embodiment of the *hieros gamos*: the coming together of opposite qualities within.

—Gloria Anzaldúa
Borderlands/La Frontera: The New Mestiza

SAI COLLAPSES IN SUCCULENT REACH SO WE ARE FINISHED AND JUST BEGINNING

In dawn's light they're bicycling by with a scarf waving and wind behind their flinted neck.

This is what I've seen through a window in my living room but what is it I am looking for?

For the up/down grades, muscles will push, pull, then turn into them and infinite others as an idea through flame.

Ghost exterior in seven colors intertwined with my routine of waking, morning, water, fruit, and tea.

They were neverhere and they're gone and I can still hear them breathe between the scrapes of any chain's rust.

If this scene is imagined impermanence let the cardinal's pause on the sweet gum branch just outside my window be too.

The bird chirps imitate the rusty chain I spoke of.

The bicycle is to get away and if they come back, I will ask: what is your good name?

I'll ask: do you wanna surya namaskar with me? If they are hungry? I'll want to know their flavor profile, favorite kinds of playlists, podcasts, games, where they're going to and from not from from what they've been reading who named them is it a dead language and what does it mean?

ARMS LINKED

SOMILA: Tranquil—no words for please or thank you

SONAL/SONALI: Golden—do it in the morning before breakfast

SUCHHAYA: Shining—kapalabhati but try not to barf

SUHAILA: Moonshine—sequence intentions meditation flow

SUNMEDHA: Intelligent—to do a common session daily

SHAKUNTALA: Brought up by birds—raja kapot opens your heart

SARASA: Swan—so does camel pose and fish's so good for hips

SHARANYA: Surrender—ringa ringa rosie ashes ashes we all fall down

CLOWNFISH ALL BORN MALE AND THEN THE DOMINANT

(SHASHA/SHEETAL *in Sir Bakasana*)

one becomes female for the purposes of reproduction

yellow-bellied water snake gives birth to litters w/out

any men anyway some cardinals like ppl all bright red

fellas and the pale of lady's gray moods when pesticide

turns common reed frog males into fully functioning fe-

males human baby born→dr. looks for a penis→she

can't find one the human baby is killed

tom boy / tom cat
masculinities report's
been high w/toxicity
but also's been here all
along like mother nature
father's horsehead husband-
ry is dedicated to play family
is to till is to plant is to
grow sri sri ram LED strike
like an insect ingathering
the day's pluck and basket
for a secure and good life
puppa labors love gives pro-
visions for needs while bro

teaches niece both salsa
dance steps and sauce ma-
king steps in the kitchen

didn't birth/seed my kids one is enby they
say parent their friend says SPILF once
wished i was dude or didn't exist both
homophobe and hate women but not like
in practice only in culture's theory like thinking
their mom can't be the man even though she is

CHILDREN'S TOY ADVERTS PROJECT ON THE WALL BEHIND

(SHASHA/SHEETAL, *still clownin'*)

Buy the boy a My Buddy doll suited in blue overalls national sales rose
for Kid Sister in the next season the girl with blonde hair a baseball cap
pigtails pink jeans or purple or yellow is an option for when

I wanted to ram my toy trucks into sister's doll house and she'd let me do it
as trade for popsicles

For a Pop Tart flavor I'd claim preference for blueberry but it wasn't true
I just wanted to seem masc same with the Monster cereals I'd ask for Boo
Berry and could have gone for the more neutral Count Chocula brown
chocolate flavor that tasted better to me but Boo Berry swayed furthest
away from the Franken Berry strawberry flavor pink I really wanted to eat

The Smurfs made it easy they were already blue and girls and boys could
both like them there was no rule that cartoon has a cat but again it was
the commercials in between on Saturday mornings I wanted My Buddy
and was too shy (Sharminda) to have the Kid Sister doll I posed my G.I.
Joe tiny soldier man green figurines humping and they'd melt in the sun I
remember my Super Soaker toy gun and swinging it like it was my dick in
the backyard

Sherwin meaning swift runner/bright friend's the name of the Cabbage
Patch Kid my mom and auntie stood outside in a store line for hours to
purchase for us I'd def rock his slacks and knit shirt 'fit in my size

ON THE BELLY, ON THE THIGH, CHEEK, ETC.

(SAJANI *pours then gleans rice from a burlap sack*)

i give a mole to every love:
the belly has one
for *s* one for *s* on
my left thigh i left
it for *s* the one on
my cheek (face) be-
longs to *s* and i can
see the one on my
arm—it's *s*'s and *s*
this one by my eye
is yours but *s*, *s*, *s*,
each one is each is

actually just for you from the missing i

feel more alive and these names mean

many things or are a system of letters
nestled together along with mine not
carved into trunks of trees i've never
seen so i cannot say so or no for sure

GLITCH OR A BLIP

(SAI *whisperstuttersings*)

the situation had deteriorated to the pot we one state had tat of oof only 754 girls for every thousand boys under the age of 7 But the on has changed since 2001 the d scuss ons of SRB, few studies on the effect of b th orde Amon the sum do but few dads stay on ted suck my sons of B, few stud cento on the effect of the ode Anon the discussions of SRB, few studies centre on the effect of the bi the d scuss ons of S B, few stud es cent e on the effect of b th o de implications have aroused considerable controversy optimistically to follow the same pattern values of mothers living (as if)—deteriorated the s tuat on has The situation has situation had the tu tu on th at on ed sex has changed The situation had dete o ated But the situation has chan ed The situation has changed the low sons c u on the few stud wow de wow babe office at fame 1978 2010 2009 but on me the effects and then and then and them

The 1982 populate on census spayed an easement see n S. B, and the subsequent census data The oval mean SRB of the families was 0.05008. (SE = 0.00046). For most who l ve n owned dwell scan the mean births overall me(a)n and for those living in not owned dwellings it amounted to k one permit cost and then and them ANOVA F = 24.726; P<0.0001). SRB declined with family size, particularly from one to two child Nonetheless, values of mothers living in exceeded those of mothers leaving on through all the analyzed family sizes (United Nations, 1955) The high potential since 2000 as stabilized at around 120 male births per year per 100 female births so the overall mean girl situation had deteriorated to the point where one, owned dwellin s few repeat stud babe wow deeds wow dude T then we have the point in all dust cats The situation bad

DIVINE/PURE BANTERS WITH HOWLS AND OTHER ANIMAL SOUNDS

Studs on the street corner light me up   I flick ash and smile back

Burned filters wedge between sidewalk panels but my daughter oh my

Daughter oh my daughter's been gone so long now I can't remember

Remember what her voice sang like when she'd sing me my lullabies

Can many things swirl calmer than sperm bursts white goo and swim to

Completion and setting and forgetting futurity cancers cells with smoke

Synthetic lipid-like molecules enter membrane walls and high my spit

SASMITA CASTS HAND SHADOWS

not breeders still come out—

for the animals fucking like bunnies like all

the time like lions in dens my my Mmamoriri name sounds

like a fox too in mothertongue howl like dogs would do

the shrimp are born girls to become men to mate the morays

only attack when provoked sometimes people are like who

wears the pants in the relationship and we're like both

and we both dress in dresses sometimes or we say they're

the cat and we are the dog when the cat's away the mice

will play will play on like the gliridae a California

dormouse mates monogamously for life but they die

young in the end anyway forever is a mighty long time

or some weeks they dress like a white bearded dad one day

then shave for a dress one to wear after pulling gently

up a tight pair of fishnets fast and relative to the moon

macaques and whiptail
lizards and bluegill sunfish
hyenas and us

i've been able to keep up with
the double dadbod standard
bulk on our basement Bowflex
can chop wood though not so
much good with tools tech elec-
tronics basic gamer guy stuff but
discipline teaches us the binary's
bullshit and fixed like a limp

SARAH TOSSES RICE AS IF JUST MARRIED

proposals
        offer   protection

shelter   a fortress   to guard
        against   security
        armors but besides
                        i've got my work

ecstatic (s)he
                says
                    to hear yes pre-

nuptial event erases

previous identities, say
                i am my mother's daughter
industry   so we agree

to destruction   see the film about

commodity work
        it's on the syllabus

        that subversive epic:
        Modern Times

remember the factory
        sequen-
ce rolls a body

through a cog
it's Charlie Chaplin's spine!

disc by disc one at a time
consequent successors

bloodline extractions [not to] demand

[not too] much protest

all the love letters left in our
Union's Lost and Found

PRONE POSES

(SID *in frog, child, bow, etc.*)

see him maybe
raise our hands
as if in supplication
frozen?disfigured? ne-
ar-dying? ~~INVISIBLE~~
in the box the boy's in
where roles locked
as in locked him face
down locked her all them

what congeals the give-and-take
from accretion? what is a family
for? what makes a house's hold
run? is there a circuit staged at
the center? a room in which to re-
enter? any wagers on the gender?!
what forms will we take? what
speech each subsequent speaks!

MOON/COOL GAZE OFF INTO THE MIDDLE DISTANCE

Who shoed the fame

now? We snatched

one fusty scab.

Oh to be tuned back to the pack!

Whey aunt sent

decays when we

stand ousted.

We took out abodes

and can fade any

focused dynasty.

SIDHANGANA'S FINISHING SCHOOL LIST

→ continuity depends on sons

→ send an appropriate thank you message to the hostess after the dinner

→ girls cannot hold prosperity in some societies so a male child is essential to retain wealth

→ salutations! & oh yes the meal on the good plates and your dress and jewelries very nice

→ his curations are selective while hers are strict or she's unorganized while he's laid back

→ women are so emotional men playing in NFL/NBA etc. are pros

→ girls are transitory members they marry and leave home

→ su su but the rice auntie made was too too salty haha-haha!

→ even when girls remain they generally earn less than boys

→ "She earned a raise telling her male boss 'I am head of household just like you. When he said, *yes, but-* I repeated myself: 'I am head of household...just...like...you.'"'

→ the family may have to produce more money when a girlchild

→ boys bring in this money when they marry adding wealth

→ yeah well my milkshake brings bum bum bum bum bum

→ a wife's status (and thus her economic security) is not consolidated until she produces a son

→ he spent more than three month's salary on a ring for me he gets me expensive gifts every holiday he bought me a big house with so many cupboards

→ the trend to small families means the parents don't want to have several girl children before having a son

→ oh my god Becky OMG Karen little bitch let's binge watch some *90-Day Fiancé*

→ ~~\`~~ ~~\`~~ ~~\`~~

WORLD WITHOUT GIRLS—

these the
odes to
take us
out when
we take you
count what's found
then nest down by
the maps and ask
the dead end when
second sons each be-
come homos
these odes take
us and you and you
and you choose many
a body hate these
odes but just why
we do not know

SAI: The Divine Person Akin to Being a God

coxcomb's eyes
shut beau mod
fop's ocean bounty
a skyed bay dashes
dandy asks: "What's
open?" my mad
tabs and a notebook

<3 sai <3

Suvali: Full of Grace

we shadow
types know
us and know
the advocated
unknown don’t
keep away
we not a man we not
a woman we came up
and cupped
hands to a
chest we we
know about you

SAII

my name's a
man's name don't
sweat my name
huff and puff
my name say ban
say upon
and at about
two a.m. say
of my name
a body bent
east/west my
namesake pushes
out puts out put
food out my book
states names
face them
they symptom
they say an
abyss that's
that's what they'd bet

bamboo on a
one   hopscotch
and spots
caste and cast
away   stacked
woman want to
keep the way
of my name
when my husband
escapes the want
on my head to
shampoo tub wet
but no   move on
odes out move
on out of town

SAJANI Sajani Beloved Sajani

mast aback he pouts
at what names the state
he catches a sway
on a peak apt to
feuds not houses
not towns not feet
the estate has went
has moved a few tones
stay as epochs fastened
to the dead end when
quotas decayed
each season hens had
waned then stoned hope
becomes the baby's face

SARAHSARAHSARAH

we nose the cement
pavement washes off
a penny on a toy
and we move out
of town mast
aback we pout
dance off
mud bottoms
each shoe mud
bottoms each paw

hahajajalolzhahajajalolz

opaque names say
us opaque names
stay us   we jump
the body on as
when face up upon
the stone we want
what mom wants
what's best to keep

mooncoolmooncoolmooncoolmooncoolmooncool
mooncoolmooncoolmooncoolmooncool
mooncoolmooncoolmooncoolmooncool
mooncoolmooncoolmooncool
mooncoolmooncoolmooncool
mooncoolmooncoolmooncool
mooncoolmooncoolmooncool

SAI CIRCLES THE REST AS THEY REST

no song no singing no silences no music...no milk no territory no
engine...no self no restoration no saying...no no terrible child no water...
no vestige no scholars no pipe...no healer no blood...no illusions no wind
no vista no luxuries...no marvel no power no need to worry worry hurry
nor sparkle...no no no no truffles no oil...no onion no fruit no frutas no
bread no class no kind...oh variety! no sort no simmer...no savor no spit
no swallow...no breathing no bedding no mattress...no blanket no fall
to the floor and sweat...no pillow no sharp objects no shirts...no problem
no pleasure no instance...no time no questions so sorrow...no daughter no
dear so disappear...no dotgov...no labor no rest no art...no brush no bush
no wickedness no split no pier...no mezzanines no yearling no driving
without a license no cowherd's son no retreat no honor no post no impasse
no kill no

STUDY (II + IIIx∞)

doctors announce times of death and sisters sleep then
spend days holed up in the library to learn words like
amniocentesis and kiss in-law cousins in blue film rooms
where the women wear no gloves and smell of blood
and marigolds where *a cat trotted down the hospital hall with*
a female fetus dangling from her mouth this is a story about
girls who were never maybe this wouldn't be acceptable
to most persons where you might be from but we're awake
for hours before we even brush our teeth or bathe some
days we talk 2U over phones and echo remember dancing
to the *I Am A Disco Dancer* song in yr mum&dad's room while
they were asleep we reread your algebra textbooks some
afternoons we tried to trace the way you make loops when
you draw out numbers like two or practice your signature

SLITHER

(CHORUS *in serpent pose then cobra then they slither)*

with their hemipenes and blanketwarm pheromones
nests of red garden snakes are

gay they gather to a ball to slither and
entwine all together

they might reproduce by doing so but they also might not give
a poke a take a bite a bout binge rampage play they may wart
blister disease bruise bacchanal group same time next week

SENTRY PROPHECIES

(SIDHANGANA *in savasana*)

upon us   tortured

deserts made   place

a young age when sisters

went missing the mess trans-

pires expires consider

the bear   or   otter   a wolf or danger

when gala   vicars sing soothing
laments

we have the body of a woman

painter sold work for a song to
echo towards evening and really hear it

ACT III
etherair

...and now you must survive because we love you,
and for the sake of your children and your children's children.

—James Baldwin
"My Dungeon Shook: Letter to My Nephew
on the One Hundredth Anniversary of Emancipation"

SAI'S CLOSET

(*in extended triangle pose chest aerial*)

Sorting through more remembered days when I found my gender some joyous ones: Was born a daughter yet there's a picture of me at about age three circa the early 1980s in which I wear a navy blue collared button up jumpsuit with a yellow necktie dyed in an orange floral print. I don't remember but am told I wanted to wear that tie every day and if I couldn't I'd throw myself on the floor in tantrum. I've also seen a picture of my second cousin at age three wearing a white and red dress just a few days before his first haircut but that was just for laughs kali haswanu matteh I'm told.

When they had to run some errands before moving from Bowling Green to DC, Jen and Evan for the first time left their firstborn alone at home with Jenny and me when he was maybe six months. We brought him a onesie welcome to this world gift with a unicorn printed on it and I have a hoodie to match, it's electric blue. Jen yelled in, "Teach him everything you know!" as she walked out the door. We started by telling baby Henry about how Prince played every instrument in all his songs and about the Love Symbol he invented and I can't remember what after that but Hank didn't cry the whole time while hanging out with just us.

The first Operation Sappho I went to was upstairs at Donny's Place that leather bar shut down now in Pittsburgh but I never went into the basement. I love that tan blazer I'd wear it for sport those days I sported so much I wore it out. Caldwell has photos from those Sappho dance parties some mounted at the Warhol I wish I still had my Gutter Glitter show clothes oh I miss those bright femme shiny short mod go-go frocks how they'd show off my swole from the miles of bicycle commutes warrior one-two-threes 11:11 kaan pakad squats and leg day work.

NO EMPIRE

(SHEETAL *hops on* SHASHA*'s back*)

Quing steps in the kitchen   Abnormal patriarchal hierarchies (Feminized men!)

My daddy she has all the skills a woman would ever need my daddy she keeps me well fed

The piggyback frog mates to the death he straddles on to grow and stays 'til he emaciates

A world without girls is darkness between predatory fireflies She's a man eater Oh just a pre-

pubescent phase to grow out of in time   Some scavenger animals have a "pseudo-

penis" and they can be cocksure killers   Bubble builder fish exponentialize each of their

genders   Three males sometimes as three   New Mexico's state lizard nips lady

ears with a jerky gait that swaggers a sway   Old World monkeys to queer our futures

pursue no depression and good rest for only homo sapiens habit sexisms even birds those cocks

don't fight flight out the nest maybe that's a typo or maybe just ask them about their pronouns

SHIULI: Flower—Sue Me
SHREETH: Best of all—Lana Filth
SHRIKA: Fortune—Surely Temple
SHRIMAYI: Fortunate—Eva Destruction
SHRIYA: Prosperity—Rosalía's "Saoko Papi"
SUCHIPATRAM: Archive—Dewy Decimated
SANTATATIKA: Progeny—Ellen Degenerate
SARAVATI: A River—Christian Sins
SAMUDRA: The Sea—Pisces Rising

IN THE DAUGHTER INDUSTRY BREEDS FANTASY

(SUVALI *under a spotlight/holding a mirror*)

In persistence not either of us has to be one or the other or only just that they are our other. As in A's despot duality as in the daughter industry breeds fantasy weddings fireworks and horses, helicopters and drums to stop the traffic. But I still love the thrill in any vidaai's barter game and the need to buy new lipstick to apply and re-apply and to receive head while wearing bright saris in the dark back rooms at reception dance parties.

What is it I am asking of you? To say an elegy by heart/to zero our dying before birth. The history of desire in so many houses says son. To know of the daughter aversion. He will be a marker/shadow our every endeavor happily. As for the girlchild say this over so many million times over now: as for the girlchild say this: convexity claims victory with that camera that can see our insides.

BURNING WIND AND WATER

(SUVALI *holds a book now while the sound of fire burning wind and water rushing comes from backstage*)

A mother's body keeps—grows and shrinks and grows and shrinks again to accomplish what's almost impossible.

It is as if each organ has become its own organization with its own leaders, its own devotees.

Her body wakes some feeling from a dream the one where all the animals on the block shed fur and feathers into the gutters and the gutters clog up.

The lungs say clean my blood and the cells say yes in blue and red.

Her body keeps channeling this one figure from a movie about a book about a recent ecological disaster and then death and walking through the desert see the mountains.

In the book a voice says *see* and *look* and *hear here I am* and *I'm here watch me here I go* and in the movie: drought and smashed glass, trees and broken concrete fill the street for the people to clean.

Few adjectives exist in the languages we have left for situating and rumor has it another sequel will soon follow.

And her body becomes a sublimate of a fracture so jagged that to think of it on skin, say, would leave no option for stitches: leave the cut so open that any idea of suture would be like a circus trying to end, pack up the tent, and leave town with no trace by midnight.

MINGLE

(SUVALI *joins* SAJANI *with the mirror, the book, the spotlight, the sounds of fire, wind, and water*)

Between livings and deads I hush up.
Ladies: who would be a daughter
sprouts lush out from river sand and
siphoned singing. Decades ago some
passage of (f)acts manifested brazenly.
Husband escaped to a movement.
He detected deformities. Our
girl's rice-sized for a moment,
for each obliteration chromosome
myriads could collide with life.
Transience subdued into bloom.
I thought: how many hands held
me since my birth? I am
iteration in place with
pacifiers, pageantry, the brooding
pink of cap and blanket
covering yellowish cover up
and case files over covered
my crucial naming, my holding,
my distinction had come to
surface at nubile and knighthood.

IS LIKE FIRE TO THE FAMILY

(SAJANI *offers* SUVALI *a warm embrace*)

For the falling through ice and light I am silentladies.

Sometime before now my acts occurred without shame: the discovery of deformities in rice, each opiate I ate at bedtime.

Put the size of my descendants in your hands for a while.

Check for any destruction that might conflict with the kind of life I said was transitory for the subject of flowers.

I am a recurrence in place for peacekeeping forces, no luxury.

The silk pink blanket meditative by fire lamp.

I have my difference/emerged through the melting.

She was never with me—I only imagined.

Her eyes may have been green or the light reflecting off the dam's concrete offers a glint for aching tumult in relentlessness newborns hold: no sleep now or later on.

We exist in land drained from the missing.

Fiercely for one another come and go sweeping floodplains we continue out.

AN APOLOGY FOR OUR MOTHERS

(SAJANI *rocks like when a lullaby*)

A pace through the bedroom when she
turns to breathe into my clavicle. My
ankle—an obtrusion of crack

and swell and so we sit rhythming
hums with sleep and then we sleep
when she becomes an inhale/ex.

Another missing girl dreams to me
at dawn. My daughter would
be an heir or her own error.

My wild unmarried braid undone again.
'Til my estrus breaths—coconut oil soothes to fray.

Her memory's a fragmented gamete
turn fontanel closed to form recognition
rattles and a coo. She could have been

dancing even to my uneven lazy beats.
But I cannot say that she disappeared
I cannot say that she was (n)everhere.

Waken and for the time being for the moment
collapse of speech and speaking. Milk sucked
out a nipple turned to powder add water. Gadgets
heat food fast for our ground exegeses to render
the workday formidable but sometimes I want
to feel like falling overnight through melting ice.

CLAMORING TO BE HEARD

(SUVALI *scratching*)

ghost girls scratch in me:
they say stop mourning
me to live on as these marks
stretch they say look so I watch
them turn nowhere into at least
one dead-end street to finish
each edge demarks any fix
which is solution enough
to say hey see ways breath
takes into account so take
a breath like my name
spill it out for the next

NAME'S A MANTRA

(SIDHANGANA *on a loop*)

S A I S A I S A I S A I S A I S A I S A I S A I S A I S

A I S A I S A I S A I S A I S A I S A I S A I S S A J A

N I S A J A N I S A J A N I S A J A N I S A J A N I S A

J A N I S A J A N I S A J A N I S A S M I T A S A S M I

T A S A S M I T A S A S M I T A S A S M I T A S A S M I

T A S A S M I T A S A R A H S A R A H S A R A H S A R A

H S A R A H S A R A H S A R A H S A R A H S A R A H S H

E E T A L S H E E T A L S H E E T A L S H E E T A L S H

E E T A L S H E E T A L S U V A L I S U V A L I S U V A

L I S U V A L I S U V A L I S U V A L I S U V A L I S U

V A L I S H A S H A S H A S H A S H A S H A S H A S H A

S H A S H A S H A S H A S H A S H A S H A S H A I V I S H A I

V I S H A I V I S H A I V I S H A I V I S H A I V I S H

A I V I S H A I V I S H A I V I S H U S H M A S H U S H

M A S H U S H M A S H U S H M A S H U S H M A S H U S H

A L U L U S H A L U L U S H A L U L U S H A L U L U S H

A L U L U S H A L U L U S H A L U L U S H A F A L I S H

A R I S O M I L A S O N A L S U C H H A Y A S U H A I L

S U N M E D H A S H A K U N T A L A S A R A S A S H A R

A N Y A S H I U I L I S H R E E T H I I I S H R I K A S

H R I M A Y I S H R I Y A S U C H I P A T R A M S A N T

A T I K A S A R A V A T I S A M U D R A S A L O N I S A

N J U L A S H A F A L I S H A R I S O M I L A S O N A L

S U C H H A Y A S U H A I L S U N M E D H A S H A K U N

T A L A S A R A S A S H A R A N Y A S H I U I L I S H R

E E T H S H R I K A S H R I M A Y I S H R I Y A S U C H

I P A T R A M S A N T A T I K A S A R A V A T I S A M U

D R A S A L O N I S A N J U L A S H A F A L I S H A R I

S O M I L A S O N A L S U C H H A Y A S U H A I L S U N

M E D H A S H A K U N T A L A S A R A S A S H A R A N Y

A S H I U I L I S H R E E T H S H R I K A S H R I M A Y
I S H R I Y A S U C H I P A T R A M S A N T A T I K A S
A R A V A T I S A M U D R A S A L O N I S A N J U L A S
U R A B S A U R A B I S O H A M S O L U L U S O S O H A
M S O H A M S O H A M S O H A M S O H A M S O H A M S O
H A M S O H A M S O H A M S O H I A M S O H A M S O H A
M S O H A M S O H A M S O F I A S O H A M S O H A M S O
H A M S O H A M S O H A M S O H A M S O H A M S O H A M
S O H A M S O H A M S O H A M S O H A M S O H A M I A M
S O H A M S O H A M I A M S O H A M S O H A M I A M S O
H A M S O H A M I A M S O H A M S O H A M I A M S O H A
M S O H A M I A M S O H A M S O H A M I A M S O H A M S
O H A M S O H A M S O H A M S O H A M S O H A M S O H A
M S O H A M S I N J I N I S I N J I N I S I N J I N I S
I N J I N I S I N J I N I S I N J I N I S I N J I N I S
I N J I N I S W A R A S Y U Y S A T V I S W A R A S Y U
Y S A T V I S V E D A S A T Y A S H A L Y A C H I K I T
S A K A H S W A R A S Y U Y S A T V I S W A R A S Y U Y
S A T V I S V E D A S A T Y A S H A L Y A C H I K I T S
A K A H S W A R A S Y U Y S A T V I S W A R A S Y U Y S
A T V I S V E D A S A T Y A S H A L Y A C H I K I T S A
K A H S A V R I T I S A V R I T I S A V R I T I S A V R
I T I S H A I L I S A U R A S H A I L I S A U R A S H A
I L I S A U R A S A I S A J A N I S H A S H A S H E E T
A L S A S M I T A S A I S U V A L I S A R A H S I D H A
N G A N A S I D H A N G A N A S I D H A N G A N A S I D
H A N G A N A S H A N T I S H A N T I S H A N T I S H A
N T I S H A N T I S H A N T I S H A N T I S H A N T I S
H A N T I S H A N T I S H A N T I S H A N T I S H A N T
I S H A N T I S H A N T I S H A N T I S H A N T I S H A
N T I S H A N T I S H A N T I S H A N T I S H A N T I S
H A N T I S H A N T I S H A N T I S H A N T I S H A N T
I S H A N T I S H A N T I S H A N T I S H A N T I S H A
N T I S H A N T I S H A N T I S H A N T I S H A N T I S

SARAH SWAYS

Ephemera in time

the pillow you left smells less like our

heads and then mine

remains here

hotel ashtrays with

grandmother's stories of stealing them year
after year

years ago
in time your blanket creases

my face's cheekskin oils itself

into threads where your hair's

been braided

in limbo left in time
the bed's foot by my feet

rocking we fall asleep

to each other's heartbeat

pay then part we
partake our oldest
occupation w/no
shame I've got
my work

wounds heal

bight and bite

a mother wakes before daybreak to make soup of boiled down bones to make soup to swallow of boiled down bones and potatoes to smoke before daybreak before children wake to whir(ring)

machines will light fires
a kitchen and riches she can demand
from the men surplus

LECTURE NOTES FOR SHASHA

In *Nina's Garden of Heavenly Delights* she can't come out so leaves town for the city to become the missing daughter while also Bobbi lives on at home as missing daughter too.

(me too/ shut it/ /down) (a bit bull w/lipstick/
he's a buffoon) (boys will be boys / lock her/room talk)

Fill in the blank with whatever language circulating in recent medias that promote more violence at us: ____________________________

(pull out cellphone and read headlines from news subscriptions and socials noting tones scale specificity etc.)

Translate text in Pushpa Kumari's Madhubani painting titled "Speaking Out Against Sex-Selective Abortion" from Sanskrit to English "if u kill unborn female then u r not father mother doctor or natural"

SID'S ALGORITHM'S PLAYLIST'S GIVING ME LIFE!

SALONI: Beautiful—The Pointer Sisters' "I'm So Excited" by Le Tigre
SANJULA: Beautiful—Rockabye Baby!'s rendition of Bowie's "Rebel Rebel"
SHRILA: Beautiful (Fool)—"I Will Always Love You" (Whitney's Dolly cover)
SURABH(I): Beauty—As SIDHANGANA sings it: Marvyn Gaye's "Sexual Healing"
SOHAM: That is I—Lip sync two Destiny's Child songs: "Survivor" and "Say My Name"

MORE OF THE FAIRYTALE

(SAJANI *gleans her rice pile again and places a grain on belly, thigh, cheek, etc.)*

She left with her prince as the way it is written. For his fortune and white horses carried feathers a flower garland tied to the red hemmed yards of silk I sewed by hand foot by foot each year she lived with me or was it in me or she was never with.

Could have been doctor   mother   lover's once   lover   drag queen   kin or my own divinations into mine own destinies a world built or manifested by pressed herbs and spices in the palm of hands repeating a mantra to happily ever afters again thank the goddesses feed her & all else light the fires.

With arrival comes seed to take in. Then the body grows it. A washed over gene pool chosen to pose as privilege. As chiseled cheekbones could cut a lip when kissed. A providence granted by land's administration and for sea.

BIODATA

DOB: ______________________________

Place/Time of Birth: ______________________________

Family tree, Birth order & Industries: ________________

Constitutions/doshas: ______________________________

Diet: ______________________________

Religions: ______________________________

Caste: ______________________________

And cast away: ______________________________

(Pre)Occupation(s) of Father: ________________________

Mother: ______________________________

Brother: ______________________________

Bhabhi: ______________________________

Cacka: ______________________________

Sister: ______________________________

Brolaw: ______________________________

Note: ours is a highly educated and cultural family from ____________. We are looking for family with modern outlook and rich culture.

Hobbies: ______________________________

Education: ______________________________

Currently working on: ______________________________

Salary: ______________________________

Family: ______________________________

Mothertongue: ______________________________

Fasting daily reading prayer: ________________________

Fetish: ______________________________

Gotra: ______________________________

Kink(s): ______________________________

Equipment(s): ______________________________

Stock: ______________________________

CHILD'S POSE & FLIP OVER TO HAPPY BABY

(CHORUS [Divine/Pure])

brother play:
that song again
the one about
the garden and
eaves on the stand
the one where
we event invention
one throw at a time

brother, play that
song again the one
where desert ghosts
stone fatherlandscapes
arid (au)(o)ral ones with
the whistles and a hum
where we whisper to whirs

this play takes place on a
surgical stage oh brother
could've been doctor by
now brother recreates
that old song once more

LOUD LOW OM ON REPEAT

(SARAH *as the others chant aum*)

living situations and associations call for a lease

a signature to say there is no way the body can't

become labor   /re\lease

the work trust affiliation's familial pictures

the desert as place to frame the factory

books state names
there on the table
with candle no. 1
burning "Give
Love" aromatherapy
lilies and citrus ylang-
ylang with orange hints
that was a gift received
from the landlord be-
fore she had to leave

DEAD MAN'S POSE

child's born and mother
cries in hospital for days

less for what child is/not/more for
all this world's got in store for her

names her daughter a boy's name
babe lifts lids to expose irises

so blue the white nurse
screams this is god's baby,

the devil's, or a ghost

in the Gulf of Mexico shrimps'
maters got exposed to oil in a spill

years ago so a swarm of grand-
spawns grow now with no eyes

ACKNOWLEDGEMENTS/NOTES

Endless gratitude to everyone at Nightboat Books. And grateful acknowledgements to the editors at *Prairie Schooner*, *POETRY*, *P-QUEUE*, *Twelfth House*, *CURA*, *The Academy of American Poets Poem-a-Day*, *Poetry Northwest*, *The Brooklyn Rail*, *The Believer*, *The Southampton Review* for publishing pieces from this work. Thanks also to The Chicago Poetry Center for making a broadside of "Seals Envelope with Spit."

Some language here has been lifted/erasured/repurposed from websites by sanskrit name, researchgate, the population reference bureau, webmd, the public library of science, drag name generator, the bbc, marriageextra.com, the economist, the womb with a view® 3d 4d hd and gender ultrasounds website, and from the sperm bank, inc. dba fertility center of california, california sperm bank clinic, est. 1980 website.

"In My Dotted Suit and No Dupatta" is an *I'm So Fine* (for KQ, ofc). Playing the role of an autocrat, Sacha Baron Cohen utters the words: "What are you having? A boy or an abortion?" in a scene from the 2012 Paramount Pictures production titled *The Dictator* ("Sasmita Proposes" also utters these inquiries). "She earned a raise telling her male boss 'I am head of household just like you. When he said, *yes, but-* I repeated myself: 'I am head of household...just...like...you.''" is from the documentary *Toni Morrison: The Pieces I Am* and is repeated here in "Sidhangana's Finishing School List." "*Clamoring to be Heard*" takes its title from a talk about ancestor ghosts by Carlos Fuentes. *we have the body of a woman* is a line from "It Is Not," a poem by Valerie Martínez and appears in "Sentry Prophecies." In "Study (II + IIIx∞)" the line "*a cat trotted down the hospital hall with a female fetus dangling from her mouth*" comes from a book by Mara Hvistendahl that's called *Unnatural Selection*. In "Lecture Notes for Shasha" the line "if u kill unborn female then u r not father mother doctor or natural" is an email my dad sent me upon my request for a rough Sanskrit to English translation of the text in Pushpa Kumari's Madhubani painting from 2011 titled "Speaking Out Against Sex-Selective Abortion" which I encountered in an internet search engine circa that same year. I can't remember what I had typed in to find it. Many of the pages in this book are in conversation with that work by Kumari.

"World Without Girls—" is a lipogram omitting the letters g, i, r, and l in pages typed out from the following texts under study on my table during the time of composition (2013-2017 roughly): Zia Jaffrey's *The Invisibles: A Tale of the Eunuchs of India*, Carmen Giménez's *Goodbye, Flicker*, Bhanu Kapil's *Schizophrene*, Dawn Lundy Martin's *Discipline*, and Kumkum Sangari's *Solid:Liquid: a (Trans)national Reproductive Formation.*

The Daughter Industry also can be a yogachoroeopoemverseplay. Seven is for Ntozake Shange's *for colored girls who have considered suicide/when the rainbow is enuf* with a thank you to Toi Derricotte. At the end of act three rights pending all the players dance with anyone who wants to in the room all Bollywoodishstyle to the song "Sheila Ki Jawani" by Sunidhi Chauhan, Vishal Dadlani, and Shekhar Ravjiani and at the overture the song "Daughter" by Four Tet plays as the players practice garba.

SOHAM PATEL WAS BORN IN THE EAST MIDLANDS OF ENGLAND AND RAISED IN THE WESTERN REGIONS OF NORTH DAKOTA. SHE IS THE AUTHOR OF THE POETRY COLLECTIONS *TO AFAR FROM AFAR* (2018), *EVER REALLY HEAR IT* (2018), WINNER OF THE SUBITO PRIZE, *ALL ONE IN THE END—/WATER* (2023), AND *THE DAUGHTER INDUSTRY* (2026). THEY CURRENTLY LIVE ON TUTELO/MONACAN LAND IN BLACKSBURG, VIRGINIA, U.S.A. WITH THEIR WIFE AND FAMILIES.

NIGHTBOAT BOOKS

Nightboat Books, a nonprofit organization, seeks to develop audiences for writers whose work resists convention and transcends boundaries. We publish books rich with poignancy, intelligence, and risk. Please visit nightboat.org to learn about our titles and how you can support our future publications.

The following individuals have supported the publication of this book. We thank them for their generosity and commitment to the mission of Nightboat Books:

Kazim Ali, Anonymous (3), Ava Aviva Avnisan, Jean C. Ballantyne, Rumeli Banik, Will Blythe, Rob Byrnes, V. Shannon Clyne, Theodore Cornwell, Gisela Gamper, Photios Giovanis, Amanda Greenberger, David Groff, Jonathan Groff, Daniel Handler, Sarah Heller, Karen Holtzman, Parag Rajendra Khandhar, Katy Lederer, Shari Leinwand, Daniel Levine, Elizabeth Madans, Ricardo Maldonado, Pooja Mehta, Ethan Mitchell, Caren Motika, Elizabeth Motika, Asker Saeed, The Leslie Scalapino - O Books Fund, Amy Scholder, Eric Suchyta, Benjamin Taylor, Mohan Trivedi, Divya Victor, Jerrie Whitfield & Richard Motika, Clay Williams

This book is made possible, in part, by grants from the New York City Department of Cultural Affairs in partnership with the City Council and the New York State Council on the Arts Literature Program.

NYC Cultural Affairs

NEW YORK STATE OF OPPORTUNITY. Council on the Arts